BRIDGE TECHNIQUE SERIES

READING THE CARDS

David Bird • Marc Smith

MASTER POINT PRESS • TORONTO

Master Point Press
331 Douglas Ave
Toronto, Ontario, Canada
M5M 1H2
(416) 781-0351 Internet www.masterpointpress.com

Canadian Cataloguing in Publication Data
Bird, David, 1946-
Reading the cards

(Bridge technique; 10)
ISBN 1-894154-34-7

1. Contract bridge — Dummy play. I. Smith, Marc, 1960-. II. Title.
III. Series: Bird, David, 1946-. Bridge technique; 10

GV1282.435.B57218 2001 795. 41'.53 C00-933107-7

Cover design and Interior: Olena S. Sullivan
Editor: Ray Lee

Printed and bound in Canada by Webcom Limited

1 2 3 4 5 6 7 07 06 05 04 03 02 01

Contents

Bridge Technique Series

Entry Management

Tricks with Trumps

Safety Plays

Eliminations and Throw-Ins

Deceptive Card Play

Planning in Suit Contracts

Planning in Notrump Contracts

Defensive Signaling

Squeezes made Simple

Planning in Defense

Reading the Cards

Tricks with Finesses

INTRODUCTION

Reading the Cards

The basis of all problem solving is processing the data to arrive at a logical conclusion. One of the great novelties, and attractions, of bridge is that the data is not all visible. During the bidding you can see only thirteen of the fifty-two cards. You gather further pieces of data by listening to the bids from around the table. When the dummy goes down you can see another thirteen cards and gradually — as each card is played — you gather further information about the hand.

To become a good dummy player, and defender, you must cultivate two main skills. You must read how the cards lie, to gain the data you need. You must then process the information logically, calculating which line of play or defense is most likely to succeed.

In this book we will concentrate on how to read the cards. Is this an easy task? Not particularly. You sometimes have to re-assess all the information at your disposal several times throughout a deal. In defense, you will constantly be counting points and shape, together with how many tricks you think declarer has so far established. Of course, you don't need to do all this work! If you prefer, you can treat bridge as social pastime, with half your mind on picking up young Jeremy from school or tomorrow night's big football game. To play the game well and to achieve success at it, however, it is a sad fact of life that some effort is required. Is it worth it? Yes!

CHAPTER • 1

Clues from the Bidding

Playing a contract is always easier if the opponents entered the bidding. Suppose you are sitting South, playing in 4♠, and West opened the bidding with a 3♡ preempt. Immediately you can place him with a likely seven-card heart suit. Suppose his opening lead is the king of hearts. It is now unlikely that he holds a side-suit singleton: he would probably have led such a card. Already you are inclined to place West with 1-7-3-2, 1-7-2-3, or 2-7-2-2 shape. After a few more tricks, you will have a complete map of his hand. You will know also that he is unlikely to hold any missing high cards outside his own suit. Such knowledge will greatly assist you in playing the hand.

Let's look straight away at a full deal where your line of play is affected by the auction:

East-West Vul.
Dealer South

	North	
	♠ 8 4 ♡ K 10 8 3 ◇ K 10 2 ♣ A 8 7 3	
♠ A J 5 2 ♡ 5 ◇ Q 9 8 4 ♣ K Q 10 5	N / W E / S	♠ Q 9 7 6 ♡ Q 7 2 ◇ 7 5 3 ♣ 9 6 2
	♠ K 10 3 ♡ A J 9 6 4 ◇ A J 6 ♣ J 4	

WEST	NORTH	EAST	SOUTH
			1♡
dbl	2NT	pass	4♡
all pass			

West leads the ♣K. How should you play this heart game?

Look at the trump suit first. Missing the queen, with a combined holding of nine cards, you would normally play for the drop. However, there are not many high-card points missing, which suggests that West is likely to hold a classic shape for his vulnerable take-out double — i.e. he will be short in hearts. This is enough to tilt the odds in favor of a finesse through the East hand.

You win the club lead with dummy's ace, play the king of trumps, and continue with a low trump to the jack. West shows out. Yes! You draw the last trump and must now decide how to play the diamond suit. Which defender is more likely to hold the ◇Q, would you say?

There are two reasons why West is a favorite to hold the diamond queen. Firstly, he held only one heart to his partner's three. He therefore has more space left to accommodate cards in the other three suits. Secondly, he will also hold most of the defenders' points. Even if you expected West and East to hold roughly the same number of diamonds, West would be more likely to hold any missing honor.

So, you cash the ace of diamonds and lead a low diamond to the ten. Once again the evidence from the bidding does not let you down. The finesse is successful and you make your game.

Here is a similar deal, where a defender has overcalled. If you feel up to a test, cover the defenders' cards and take over from South.

Both Vul.
Dealer East

	North	
	♠ K 9 2 ♡ 7 6 5 3 ♢ K 7 5 2 ♣ 8 7	
West ♠ 4 ♡ A K 10 9 4 ♢ Q 9 4 ♣ A 10 4 2	N / W E / S	**East** ♠ Q 6 5 ♡ J 8 ♢ J 10 8 3 ♣ Q 9 5 3
	♠ A J 10 8 7 3 ♡ Q 2 ♢ A 6 ♣ K J 6	

WEST	NORTH	EAST	SOUTH
		pass	1♠
2♡	2♠	pass	4♠
all pass			

Yes, 4♠ was an overbid. Still the game has some play. West begins the defense by playing the king, ace and ten of hearts, East discarding a club. How would you play the contract?

You ruff the third round of hearts and see that you can afford only one loser in the club suit. You cross to the king of diamonds and lead a club, East following low. Which defender is more likely to hold the ♣A, would you say?

It is West, because he is the player who entered the bidding. As he made a vulnerable two-level overcall on a five-card suit, he is a strong favorite to hold the ace of clubs. You therefore play the club jack from hand and are pleased to see this draw the ace.

When West persists with a fourth round of hearts, East throws another club and you ruff in the South hand. What now?

You play the ♣K, drawing the queen from East, and lead a third club. East surely has no more clubs and you must decide whether to ruff your last loser with the nine or the king. The choice depends on which defender you think is more likely to hold the queen of trumps. What would your decision be?

West has shown up with nine cards in hearts and clubs, East with only six. Since East has seven spaces remaining to West's four, he is more likely to hold spade length and, therefore, the spade queen. You ruff with the king and lead the ♠9. When East follows with a low card, you underplay with your eight, leaving the lead in dummy. You repeat the trump finesse, draw East's last trump, and claim. Another success for overbidding!

When an opponent has opened 1NT, you will have a very accurate picture, both of his points and his approximate shape. The best line of play on the next deal is made clear by West's opening bid. Try your skill as declarer by covering the East-West cards.

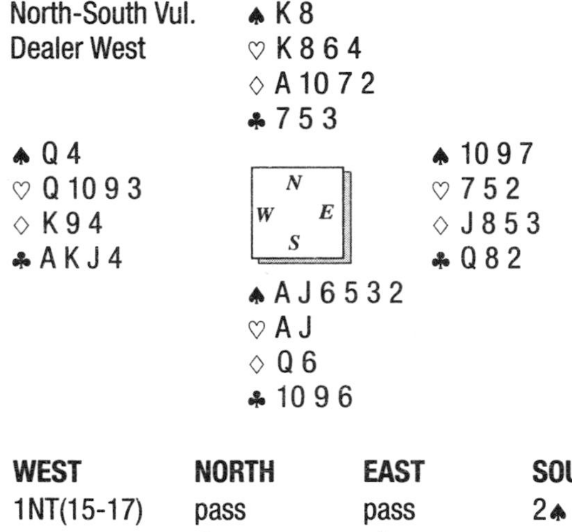

North-South Vul.
Dealer West

North: ♠ K 8 ♡ K 8 6 4 ♢ A 10 7 2 ♣ 7 5 3

West: ♠ Q 4 ♡ Q 10 9 3 ♢ K 9 4 ♣ A K J 4

East: ♠ 10 9 7 ♡ 7 5 2 ♢ J 8 5 3 ♣ Q 8 2

South: ♠ A J 6 5 3 2 ♡ A J ♢ Q 6 ♣ 10 9 6

WEST	NORTH	EAST	SOUTH
1NT(15-17)	pass	pass	2♠
pass	4♠	all pass	

North knows that you are a fine dummy player but, even so, his leap to the spade game is a marked overbid. West leads ace, king and another club to his partner's queen. Back comes the ♠10. How will you play the hand?

The North and South hands hold 22 points between them, leaving 18 points for the defenders. West's opening bid promised at least 15 points, leaving at most 3 points for East. Since he has already shown up with the ♣Q, the only other honor that East can hold is the jack of diamonds.

A trump finesse is doomed to fail, so you will have to play to drop West's queen doubleton. Even if you get lucky in that direction, you will still be one trick short. How about winning the trump switch with dummy's king and finessing the ♡J?

Once again, you know from the bidding that such a finesse is certain to lose. Can you see any other chance?

If West holds four hearts, he can be caught in a simple squeeze. You win the trump switch with the king and cross to the ace of trumps, pleased to see the queen fall on your left. After drawing the last trump, you play the ace and king of hearts, then ruff a heart. When you run your remaining trumps, West will have no good discard on the last round. As West has to discard before the dummy, you can wait and see what he throws before pitching from dummy. If he releases his ♡Q, dummy's ♡8 will score. If instead he bares the ◇K, you will make two diamond tricks. (Play the deal through with a deck of cards if you found this hard to follow.)

Clues from the bidding will often affect your play of the key suit. See what you make of this deal:

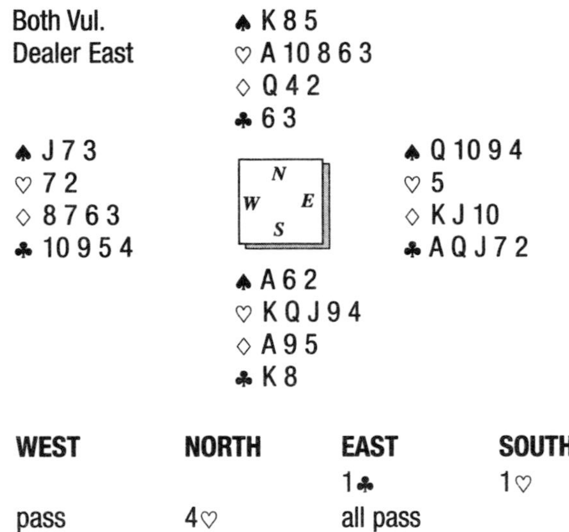

WEST	NORTH	EAST	SOUTH
		1♣	1♡
pass	4♡	all pass	

West leads the ♣10 to East's ace. You win the club continuation with the king and draw trumps in two rounds. The duplication of shape means that you are in danger of losing four tricks in spite of the 10-card trump fit and a combined 26 HCP.

Your best chance of avoiding two diamond losers lies in forcing the defenders to open the suit. Your next move is therefore to play off the top spades and exit with the third round of the suit. If East wins, you can claim your contract. However, West's ♠J takes the trick and he leads the ◇3.

If West holds the ♢K, you have a choice of winning plays — rise with the queen immediately or win the ace and lead a second diamond towards dummy's queen. With no clue to the location of the ♢K, this second option is probably the best shot, since it will also succeed if East began with a doubleton king of diamonds. (He would capture your ♢Q but would then have to concede a ruff-and-discard.)

However, East opened the bidding and has shown up with only nine points at most outside the diamond suit (♣A-Q-J and perhaps the ♠Q). It is therefore extremely likely that he holds the ♢K. Can you see how to take advantage of this information?

When you play a low diamond from dummy, East plays the ten. Allowing him to win this trick leaves him endplayed. Whether he leads away from his presumed ♢K next or plays a black card for a ruff-and-discard, you will restrict your losers to one in each side suit.

Look for a similar play on the next deal:

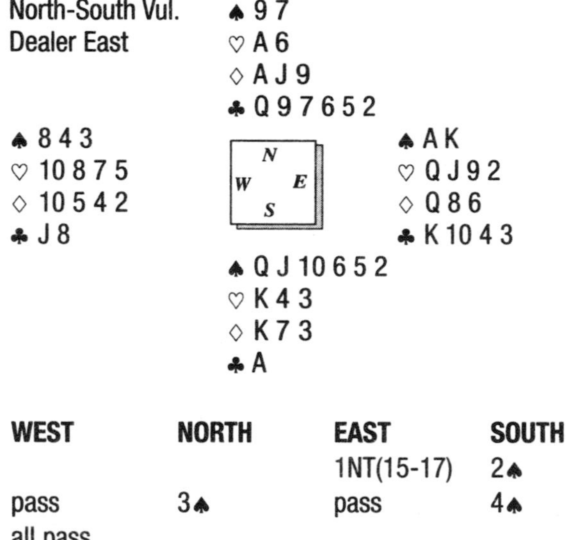

West chooses just the right time for a trump lead. East wins and draws a second round, depriving you of your heart ruff. How should you play when East switches to the ♡Q at Trick 3?

You win the heart switch with the king and draw the last trump from the West hand. Since East held only two spades, it is no good hoping to ruff out a doubleton ♣K from his hand. Nor is any squeeze possible, since East sits over your threats. You will therefore have to play the diamond suit yourself.

The defenders started with sixteen points between them. West can hold at most one jack and East is therefore marked with the ♢Q. You cross to the ♡A and lead the ♢J from dummy, intending to run the card. If East covers with the queen, you win with the king and finesse dummy's ten on the way back. This 'backward finesse', as it is called, is a 50% prospect once you know that East holds the queen. Justice is done on this occasion and you make your game.

Detective work

When you have a key decision to make in one suit, it may be best to play on the other suits first. By discovering how the high cards lie there, you can improve your chance of guessing correctly in the first suit.

Here is a simple example of the technique:

Neither Vul. Dealer West	♠ J 10 8 6 ♡ J 8 3 ♢ K 7 2 ♣ K 8 6	
♠ K ♡ A K Q 6 4 ♢ 10 6 5 4 ♣ J 3 2	 N W E S	♠ 7 5 2 ♡ 9 7 2 ♢ A 9 3 ♣ 10 9 7 5
	♠ A Q 9 4 3 ♡ 10 5 ♢ Q J 8 ♣ A Q 4	

WEST	NORTH	EAST	SOUTH
1♡	pass	pass	1♠
pass	2♠	pass	4♠
all pass			

With a great hand for a fourth-seat 1♠ overcall, you leap to game on the second round. West cashes two hearts and continues with the heart queen, which you ruff. What next?

Many players would cross to the ♣K and take a trump finesse. 'No reason why East shouldn't hold the king,' they would say. The finesse loses and they go one down. A better idea, at Trick 4, is to play a diamond to dummy's king. As it happens, East wins with the ace. Can he hold the trump king now? No! With seven points he would have responded to the opening bid. So, you should take your only chance — to drop the ♠K singleton. The gods are with you on this occasion and you make the game.

On the next deal the contract depends on a two-way guess for a queen. East has opened 1NT, so you must count his points in the other suits to see if he is likely to hold the missing queen.

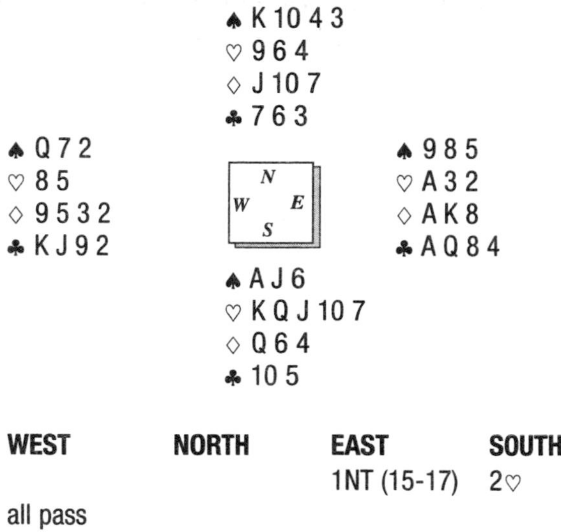

WEST	NORTH	EAST	SOUTH
		1NT (15-17)	2♡
all pass			

West leads the ♣2 against your partscore in hearts. East wins with the ace and returns the ♣4 to West's jack. When West continues with the ♣K, you ruff in the South hand.

Are the first few tricks already a blur? On many deals, success will depend on keeping track of the high cards that the defenders have played. This is one of them! You know that East started with 15-17 HCP and you should remember that he has shown up with six points in clubs. You knock out the ace of trumps (East has now shown up with ten points) and win the trump return. You draw the outstanding trump, then gaze thoughtfully at the spade suit. Success depends on how you read the lie of that suit. Who will you play for the missing queen?

You cannot tell who has the spade queen until you have discovered who holds the missing diamond honors, so you should play on that suit next. East wins with the king of diamonds and plays another club, forcing your last trump as West follows suit. Since there are no more clubs out, it is safe to knock out the other diamond honor. When East wins the second round of diamonds, he has shown up with seventeen points outside spades. It is not possible for him to hold the ♠Q too, so you finesse West for that card and make your contract.

Suppose West had shown up with the ace or king of diamonds. East would then hold at most fourteen points outside the spade suit, so he would be marked with the ♠Q. You would then take the spade finesse the other way.

Perhaps you are a gambler at heart and like guessing two-way finesses? Good players hate having to guess.

Clues when a defender has not bid

If a defender has passed at some stage in the auction, this may give you as much useful information as an actual bid would have done. Suppose West opens 1♡, your partner passes and so does East. If you end up as declarer, it will be reasonable for you to assume that East does not hold as many as six points.

You can make use of such an assumption on this deal:

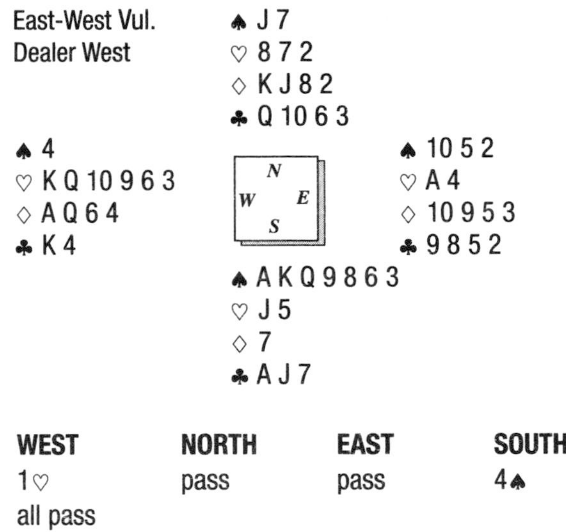

WEST	NORTH	EAST	SOUTH
1♡	pass	pass	4♠
all pass			

West leads the ♡K, East overtaking with the ace and returning a heart to the jack and queen. When West perseveres with the ♡10, East throws a club and you ruff in the South hand. How should you continue?

One possibility is to reach dummy with the jack of trumps and to finesse in clubs. However, East could not summon a response to the opening bid and has already shown up with the ace of hearts. There is therefore no chance at all of that line succeeding. Running the spade suit, hoping for an end-play, will not work either. West will reduce his hand to ♡9 ◇A ♣K4. What else can you try?

Only one line will work. You must draw one round of trumps, hoping that this exhausts West of the suit. You then lead a diamond towards dummy. If West plays low, you can win with the king, draw trumps, and subsequently give up a club. If instead West rises with the ace he will be endplayed. A diamond return will allow you to finesse the jack (you know from West's failure to respond that he cannot hold the ◇Q). A club return will be into your tenace and a heart return will give a ruff-and-discard. In both the latter cases your remaining club can be thrown on the ◇K.

Has anything else occurred to you about this deal? The defenders had various chances to break the contract. East could have switched to a club when in with the heart ace. West might also have cashed the ace of diamonds before playing a third round of hearts.

On the next deal the key decision is in diamonds. How will you give yourself the maximum chance of success?

Both Vul.
Dealer North

North:
♠ 7 2
♡ 10 5 3 2
◇ K J 8 2
♣ K Q 4

West:
♠ Q J 10 8 6
♡ 9 7
◇ Q 6 4
♣ A 7 3

East:
♠ K 9 4
♡ J 4
◇ A 10 9 5
♣ 9 8 6 2

South:
♠ A 5 3
♡ A K Q 8 6
◇ 7 3
♣ J 10 5

WEST	NORTH	EAST	SOUTH
	pass	pass	1♡
pass	3♡	pass	4♡
all pass			

West leads the ♠Q against your heart game. You win the second round of spades, draw trumps in two rounds and ruff a spade, the king appearing from East. All depends on how you guess the diamonds. Will you play to the king or to the jack?

First you must do some detective work in clubs, to see who holds the ace. As it happens, West has that card. You already place West with five good spades. If he held two aces in addition he would surely have overcalled 1♠, even when vulnerable. You therefore play a diamond to the jack, playing West for the queen rather than the ace.

Suppose instead that East had turned up with the ♣A. That would give him eight points outside the diamond suit. With the ◇A in addition he might well have opened the bidding. You would therefore place West with the diamond ace and play a diamond to the king.

Key points

1. A player who has advertised length in one or more suits during the auction is likely to be short in your trump suit when you end up playing the contract. With four trumps missing to the queen, you should normally finesse the other defender for the queen.

2. A player who opens the bidding suggests a certain number of high-card points. Usually he will hold at least twelve points (unless he has an unusually distributional hand). This knowledge is a great advantage when you play the contract. The defender who opened is a strong favorite to hold any missing honor. An opening bid of 1NT is a particularly accurate guide to the lie of the cards.

3. When a defender has chosen not to open the bidding, or has failed to respond to partner's opening bid in a suit, his point count is limited. As declarer you can take advantage of this knowledge when you plan the play.

4. When a defender has opened with a preempt, or shown a two-suiter (by bidding the Unusual Notrump or making a Michaels cuebid), a lead of the remaining side suit will usually be a singleton. Base your play on that assumption.

QUIZ

A.

	♠ J 9 4 2
	♡ K J 5 3
	◇ 10 7 4
	♣ 8 5
◇8 led	N / W E / S
	♠ K Q 10 8 7
	♡ A 2
	◇ A J 2
	♣ K J 3

WEST	NORTH	EAST	SOUTH
	pass	pass	1♠
pass	2♠	pass	4♠
all pass			

West leads the ◇8 against your spade game. You capture East's queen with the ace and lead the king of trumps. East takes with the ace, cashes the king of diamonds and leads another diamond. You are fearful of a ruff but West follows suit. How will you continue?

B.

	♠ Q J 6 5
	♡ A J 6
	◇ 9 7 3
	♣ J 9 2
◇A led	N / W E / S
	♠ A K 8 7 3 2
	♡ K 10 3
	◇ 4
	♣ Q 10 4

QUIZ

WEST	NORTH	EAST	SOUTH
1NT(15-17)	pass	pass	2♠
pass	3♠	pass	4♠
all pass			

West leads the ◇A against your spade game, East following with the two. You ruff West's ◇K continuation. How will you guess the hearts?

C.

♠ J 7 3
♡ A J 5
◇ A K 7 3
♣ 8 7 4

♣A led

N / W E / S

♠ A K 10 9 6 4
♡ K 8 2
◇ J 10
♣ J 5

WEST	NORTH	EAST	SOUTH
			1♠
2♣	dbl	pass	2♠
pass	4♠	all pass	

West cashes the ace and king of clubs and continues with the club queen. East throws a heart on the third round and you ruff in hand. Both defenders follow to the ace of trumps. What is the most likely lie of the trump suit? Will you finesse in trumps or play for the drop?

QUIZ

D.

	North	
	♠ 9 7 5 ♡ A 8 4 ◇ Q 7 2 ♣ 9 6 5 3	
◇J led	W N E S	
	♠ A Q ♡ K Q J 9 6 2 ◇ 8 5 3 ♣ K J	

WEST	**NORTH**	**EAST**	**SOUTH**
		1◇	1♡
pass	2♡	all pass	

The defenders take three tricks in diamonds, West throwing a spade on the third round. East then switches to a low club. Will you play the king or the jack?

Answers

A. A successful heart finesse, or ruffing out the heart queen, will be worth nothing. Success depends solely on guessing the club position. If East holds the ♣A, you need to play a club to the king. If instead East holds the ♣Q, you must play a club to the jack. Which is it to be? East has shown up with nine points in spades and diamonds. If he held the ♣A too that would give him a total of thirteen points and he would have opened the bidding. You should therefore play a club to the jack.

B. It seems from East's two of diamonds at Trick 1 (a discouraging card) that West holds A-K-Q in the suit. After drawing trumps you should play on clubs to discover how the missing honors in that suit lie. If West holds both the ace and king, this will bring his point-count to 16. He will not have room for the heart queen and you should therefore finesse East for that card. If instead West turns up with only the ace of clubs, he will need the heart queen to bring his total within the 15-17 point range. You will therefore finesse against West in hearts.

C. Since West has overcalled, and holds six clubs to his partner's two, the odds favor East holding Q-x-x in the trump suit. Should you therefore cross to dummy and take a trump finesse? No, because if East does hold the trump queen you can guarantee the contract by playing king and another trump. If East wins the third round with the queen he will have to open one of the red suits, giving you a tenth trick. Reading the most likely lie of the cards is one thing. You must still think of the deal as a whole and calculate the best play to deal with any lie of the cards.

D. There are eighteen points out, so there is room for West to hold the ace of clubs. However, he will surely not hold the ace of clubs and the king of spades. This would mean East had opened on a ten-count and West had refrained from some sort of response when holding eight points and at least four spades. You should therefore rise with the king of clubs. If this loses to West's ace, you can be sure that a subsequent spade finesse will succeed.

CHAPTER • 2

Reading the Opening Lead

You will have heard the saying 'many a contract is lost at Trick 1'. It's true! Some declarers go through their entire bridge life making the same clear-cut mistakes time and again. Look at this elementary situation:

	◇ K 8 4 2	
◇ Q J 10 7	N / W E / S	◇ A 9 5
	◇ 6 3	

West leads the ◇Q against a major-suit game. 'King, please,' says declarer. What is the point of that? There is not a chance in 100 that West has led the queen from A-Q-J. East is certain to hold the ace and it is nearly always right to play low from dummy. The defenders can take the two tricks that are their due, but you will later have the chance to ruff out East's ace, establishing the king.

A similar situation can arise in notrump:

You are in 3NT and West leads the ♠Q. Now, in a notrump contract, it is possible that he is leading from A-Q-J-10-x. There is no problem on the first trick — you should play low. When West continues with the ♠J, you have a guess to make. If East started with ace doubleton or third, you will do best to play low again. Only if West has A-Q-J-x(-x) will it cost you to play low on the second round. With five good spades West would often have entered the auction. With A-Q-J fourth, West might have chosen to lead a different suit. On balance you will do best to hold up the king on the second round too.

The opening lead provides considerable information about the defensive hands. The card led will often reveal the location of missing high cards in that suit. This information, whilst very useful in itself, is only the tip of the iceberg. Sometimes, the opening lead will locate most, or even all, of the missing honors in the other suits. Cover the East-West hands on the next deal:

North-South Vul.
Dealer West

North:
♠ Q J 4
♡ A Q 10 5
◇ J 6 4
♣ J 9 8

West:
♠ 10 9
♡ J 9 6 3
◇ A Q 2
♣ K Q 7 2

East:
♠ 6 5 3
♡ 8 4
◇ K 8 7 5
♣ 10 6 4 3

South:
♠ A K 8 7 2
♡ K 7 2
◇ 10 9 3
♣ A 5

WEST	NORTH	EAST	SOUTH
1NT	pass	pass	2♠
pass	3♠	pass	4♠
all pass			

West's 1NT opening is weak, showing 12-14 HCP. He leads the ♠10 and you draw trumps in three rounds. What now?

You need four heart tricks to bump your total to ten. You begin with the ace and king, then lead a third round towards dummy, West following with the nine. Should you finesse or play for the drop?

The defenders started with 15 points between them, so the opening bid gives no direct clue about the position of a missing jack. Look back to West's opening lead, however. Would he have led a trump if he held the ace and king of diamonds? It's unlikely. Most defenders cannot wait to lead an ace-king combination. It is a near certainty that East holds the king of diamonds and that means that the remaining twelve points are all with West. You finesse dummy's ♡10 and emerge triumphantly with ten tricks.

Let's take a look at other types of information that the opening lead may reveal about the leader's hand. Suppose, for example, that you receive the lead of a low spot-card against a trump contract. It is a reasonable assumption that the opening leader does not hold the ace-king or any strong honor combination in an unbid side suit.

On many occasions the opening lead will give you a two-way guess. How many times have you faced this situation?

	♢ Q 10 6	
♢ K 9 7 2	N W E S	♢ J 8 5 3
	♢ A 4	

You are in a suit slam with an ace missing elsewhere. West's opening lead is the ♢2 and you must guess whether to play the queen or the ten from dummy. What is your reaction?

To some extent the answer depends on the quality of the player sitting West. Good bridge players will often lead away from a king, particularly against a suit slam, but hate leading from a jack. If you rate West as a sound performer, you should therefore play the queen from dummy.

If West is a weak player, he may well be terrified of leading away from a king but he may not appreciate the dangers of leading from a jack. Against such an opponent, you would do better to call for dummy's ten. Indeed, if West is someone whom you don't like, you can insult him by calling for the ten! It may cost you the contract, through.

You have a two-way guess here, too:

♢ K 8

♢ Q 10 5 3 — N / W E / S — ♢ A 9 7 6

♢ J 4 2

You are playing in 6♡, with all suits solid except for the diamond suit. West leads the ♢3. Should you play the king from dummy or not?

Almost always you should play low. Defenders very rarely underlead an ace. They often lead from a queen. Even if the bidding to the slam has made it likely that the ♢K may be in dummy (when West might well decide to underlead the ace), it is not right to put up the king. West would lead low from the queen, too, so it is as least as good to play low.

When the opening lead proves to have been from a risky holding, you may conclude that the defender had equally awkward holdings in the other suits. Suppose West leads a low diamond against your 4♠ contract and it subsequently turns out that he held J-x-x-x or Q-x-x in the suit. Most defenders would prefer not to lead from holdings such as these if they have a safer alternative. You can therefore infer that he has similarly unattractive holdings, such as A-x-x-x, in the other side suits.

Let's see a full deal where you can use this type of inference:

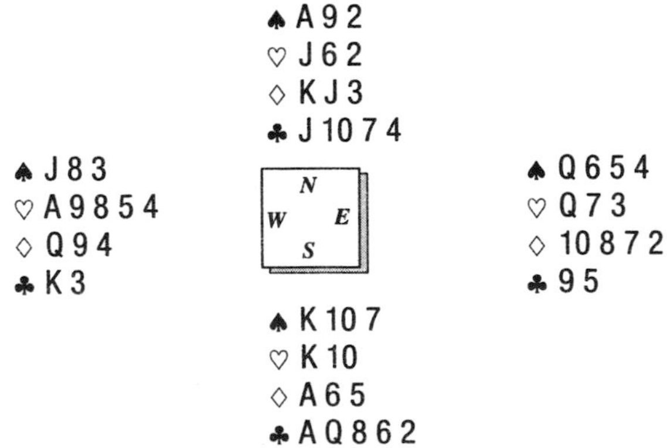

You reach a rather inelegant five club contract, bypassing the more likely-looking 3NT. West leads the three of spades and you capture East's queen with your king. A diamond to the jack wins and you run the jack of clubs to West's king.

West exits with a second trump and East follows suit. You successfully finesse West for the jack of spades and cash the ace. Then come the top diamonds, West following with the nine and then the queen. When you then re-enter dummy with a third round of trumps, West pitches a heart and East releases the thirteenth spade.

Now all you have to do is guess the hearts. You lead the jack from dummy, hoping to tempt East into a cover, but he follows smoothly with a low heart. Will you run the jack, playing East for the queen, or rise with the king, hoping that he holds the ace?

The most telling clue came all the way back at Trick 1. West's lead of a low spade from ♠J-x-x cost his side a trick in the suit. Leads from such holdings are apt to do exactly that, so why did West choose a spade? What else has he shown up with?

He had ♢Q-9-x, an equally unattractive holding from which to lead, and a doubleton king of trumps. With the spade, diamond and club leads all unappealing, West would surely have led a heart if he held queen fifth in the suit. The fact that he preferred to lead a spade implies that he holds the ace of hearts rather than the queen. With ace fifth in hearts, he would naturally look elsewhere for his opening lead.

It is therefore clear to run the jack of hearts. West may hold both the ace and queen, in which case you will go down. If the honors are split, though, you are a heavy favorite to find East with the queen and to make your contract.

The Rule of Eleven

Most defenders lead the fourth best card from a suit containing an honor (unless they have a sequence of honors). This allows declarer to make certain calculations as to the position of other cards in the suit.

	North	
	♢ A Q J 2	
West		**East**
♢ K 10 8 7 4	N / W E / S	♢ 6
	♢ 9 5 3	
	South	

After an auction of 1NT-3NT, West leads the ♢7. Subtracting the value of the card led from 11 tells declarer that there are four cards higher than the seven in the other three hands. Since he can see them all (A, Q, J, 9) in his own hand and the dummy, he knows that East cannot beat the seven. It is therefore safe for declarer to run the opening lead to his nine. Two later finesses in the suit will allow him to score four diamond tricks.

Although in this book we are concerned only with reading the cards from declarer's seat, the Rule of Eleven can be used also by the defender in the third seat. Here East can see three cards higher than the seven in the dummy, so he knows that declarer must have one such card in his hand. Not that this helps him much here!

Suppose the bidding goes 1NT-3NT and West leads the ♠2. What inference can you draw? Since the two is West's fourth best spade, he must hold a four-card suit. 'Obviously!' you may be saying, but many bridge players go to their graves without ever realizing this simple fact. That knowledge is valuable on deals such as this:

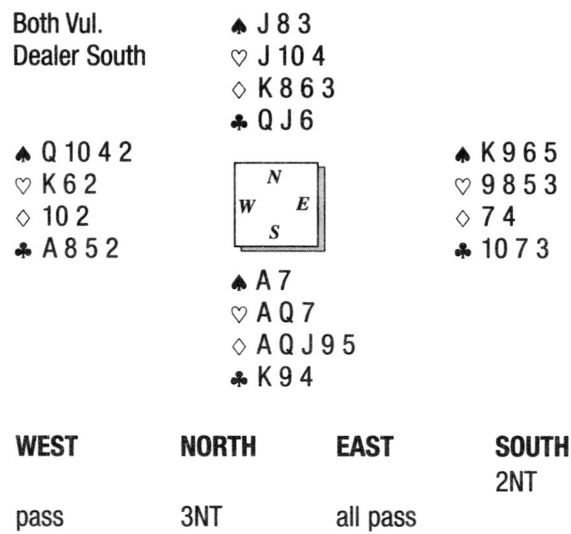
Both Vul.
Dealer South

	North	
	♠ J 8 3 ♡ J 10 4 ◇ K 8 6 3 ♣ Q J 6	
West ♠ Q 10 4 2 ♡ K 6 2 ◇ 10 2 ♣ A 8 5 2		**East** ♠ K 9 6 5 ♡ 9 8 5 3 ◇ 7 4 ♣ 10 7 3
	South ♠ A 7 ♡ A Q 7 ◇ A Q J 9 5 ♣ K 9 4	

WEST	NORTH	EAST	SOUTH
			2NT
pass	3NT	all pass	

West leads the ♠2. How would you play the hand?

Perhaps at your local club you are accustomed to playing low from the dummy. East misdefends by playing the king, rather than the nine, and you then have a second stopper in the suit. Since West would have led the 10 from a holding headed by K-10-9 or Q-10-9, you know that East must hold the ten or the nine. Any reasonable defender will play this card at Trick 1 if you play low from dummy. So your only genuine play for a second spade trick is to rise with dummy's jack, hoping that the lead is from the K-Q.

This play brings no dividend on this occasion, East covering with the king. Since no switch is dangerous, it costs you nothing to duck. East's return of the ♠5 confirms your view that the spades are 4-4. What now?

You can count seven top tricks — five diamonds and two major-suit aces. You should play on clubs for the extra tricks you need, expecting to lose only three spades and the ace of clubs. A heart finesse would be a needless risk. If it lost, you would go one down.

Suppose, still with the same North-South cards, that the spade suit was distributed like this:

West would now lead the ♠4. You would note that the two is missing, so West might have five spades. Again you try dummy's jack to no avail, East covering with the king. Back comes the ♠9, suggesting that spades are indeed 5-3. You win the second round with the ace and know now that you will go down if you knock out the ace of clubs. With spades 5-3, you must play differently, taking the heart finesse. A 50% chance is better than none!

Sometimes the Rule of Eleven allows declarer to conclude that the opening lead must be from a short suit:

♠ K 5 2

♠ 9 7 3 — N / W E / S — ♠ Q J 10 6

♠ A 8 4

West's method is to lead the fourth best card from a good suit, the second best from a poor suit. Here he leads the ♠7 against 3NT and you win East's ten with the ace. How does the suit lie?

If West's seven was a fourth best card from a good suit, he would hold Q-J-9-7(-x). Most players lead the queen from that holding, so the lead is probably from shortness.

How might such knowledge help you? Cover the East-West cards on the next deal:

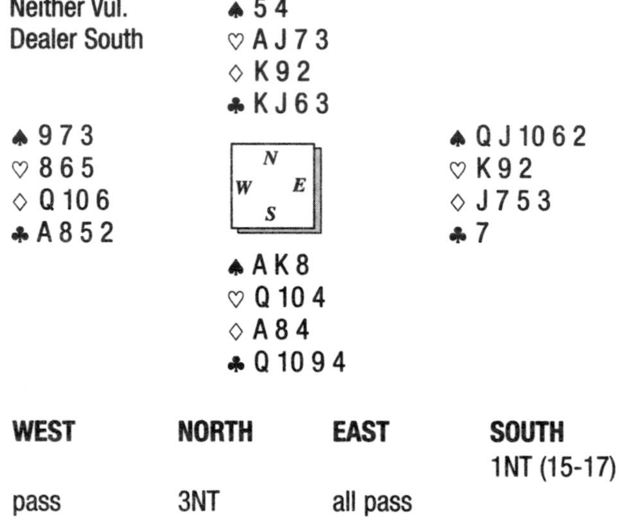

West leads the ♠7 and East plays the ten. Plan the play.

The first hurdle must be overcome at Trick 1. You should win the first round of spades, since a diamond switch might be dangerous. Now it is time to set about amassing nine tricks, and to do so you may need to knock out both the ♡K and the ♣A.

To succeed when spades are 5-3, you will have to remove the stopper that lies with the long spades first. As we have already seen, the Rule of Eleven allows you to place the long spades with East, if anyone. You should therefore run the ♡Q at Trick 2.

As it happens, the finesse loses. East returns the queen of spades, confirming your reading of that suit. You duck the second round of spades, win the third, and then play on clubs. As West has the club ace and no spade to play, the contract is secure.

Play the hand through again, knocking out the club ace first. You will go down. West will win and clear the spade suit. No endplay on East is possible and eight tricks will be the limit.

Diagnosing an impending ruff

When a defender who has bid one or more suits then leads a different side suit, you should always be suspicious. The chances are high that the lead is a singleton and he is hoping for a ruff. Look at this deal from declarer's seat:

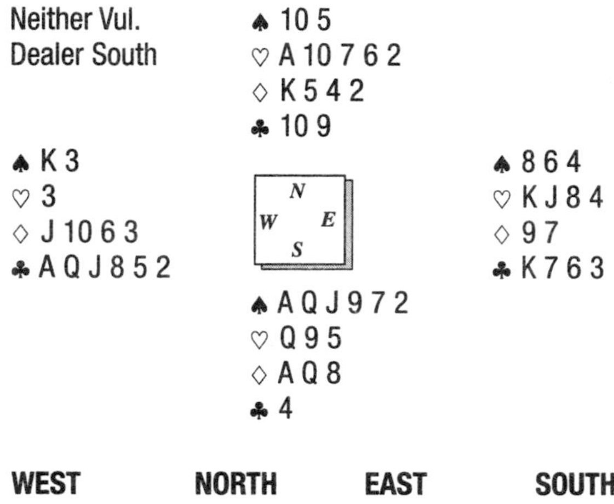

WEST	NORTH	EAST	SOUTH
			1♠
2♣	dbl	3♣	3♠
pass	4♠	all pass	

How would you play this game when West leads the ♡3?

West's clubs have been supported and an opening lead in that suit is what you might have expected. A heart lead is doubly suspicious because North's negative double indicated hearts. Why should West lead a heart from a holding such as ♡K-8-3 when he knows there are fair hearts sitting over him? He wouldn't do it. You can be sure that the lead is a singleton.

Let's see what will happen if you carelessly play low from dummy at Trick 1. East will win with the king of hearts and return the ♡4 — his lowest card in the suit, to indicate a re-entry in clubs. West will ruff and underlead his ace of clubs to put East on lead again. In with the king of clubs, East will deliver another heart ruff. One down.

The first step on the road to ten tricks is to rise with dummy's ace of hearts at Trick 1. Suppose you now take a trump finesse. West will win with the king and, as before, underlead in clubs. East will win with the club king, cash the king of hearts and give his partner a ruff. You will still go one down.

The second step on the road to ten tricks is to play ace and another trump after winning with the heart ace. West cannot score a ruff now and you make the game easily. Indeed, there is little point in a trump finesse because West is a strong favorite to hold the trump king once you have placed the heart honors with East.

You should never lose sight of the fact that information may be available to you but not to one of the defenders. The opponents' bidding helps you on the next deal but you will still need to be wide awake to take advantage. Look at all four hands and see if you can spot how declarer might bring home this apparently hopeless contract:

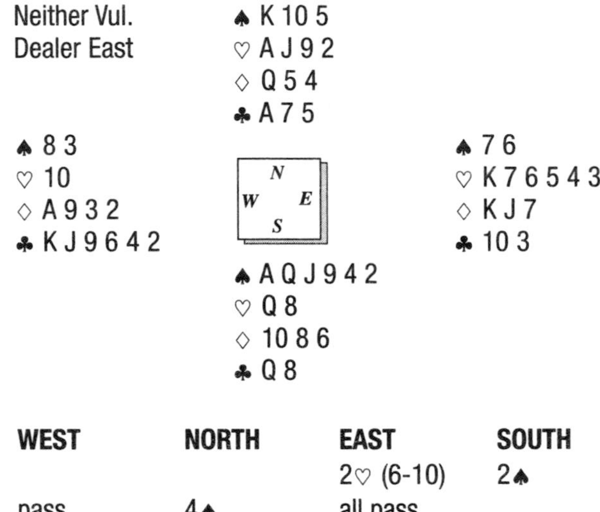

WEST	NORTH	EAST	SOUTH
		2♡ (6-10)	2♠
pass	4♠	all pass	

North might have tried 3NT but, knowing how well you play the cards, he raised to what seems to be a hopeless spade game. How would you play the contract when West leads the ♡10?

It is apparent from your South seat that the ten of hearts is a singleton. If you finesse, East will win with the king, deliver the ruff with a suit-preference card asking for a diamond return, and you will quickly be two down.

The alternative seems to be to take the ♡A, draw trumps, and concede a trick to the king of hearts. By then, though, it will be obvious to East that there is no hope for the defense if his partner does not hold the ace of diamonds. Can you see how declarer might play to deflect East from the winning defense?

Go back to the opening lead. Even without East's opening bid, it would be a clear signpost to the location of the heart king. Now think about things from East's point of view. The lead gives him similar information — it tells him that you hold the heart queen. What it does not tell him, though, is who holds the eight of hearts. You know that the heart ten is a singleton. So, too, will East if you show him your eight at Trick 1.

You should win the ace of hearts and follow with the queen from your hand. By drawing trumps ending in the dummy and then leading the low heart, you give East a problem. If he plays low, your eight of hearts will win. You can then re-enter dummy in trumps and take the ruffing finesse against East's heart king to establish a discard for one of your minor-suit losers.

Information from the bidding, the opening lead and the early play will often help you to locate the defenders' high cards. Remember that the defenders are each doing much the same kind of thing. Always be aware that the cards you choose to play can help them in this respect. Although two touching cards such as a king and queen have the same trick-taking potential, the information they give to the opponents may differ enormously. Concealing your strength or your shape from the defenders cannot cost and may reap unexpected rewards.

Key points

1. When the opening lead is a low card and you are faced with a king-jack guess, play for the leader to hold the queen. When you are faced with a queen-ten guess, play for a good player to have led from the king. A less strong player is more likely to have led from a jack.

2. The Rule of Eleven: by subtracting the value of the fourth-best opening lead from eleven, you can determine how many cards of higher rank are held by the other three players. Since you can see two of the other three hands, you can determine how many higher cards the remaining hand holds. This rule often reveals whether the lead is fourth-best from strength or second-best from weakness. It may be used by both declarer and by the defender in the third seat.

3. The opening lead combined with the early play will usually tell you how the suit led is breaking. In a notrump contract, you will then know how many winners the defenders have to cash. This information will often affect your play in other suits as it will let you know whether you can afford to lose the lead.

4. When the defenders have bid and supported a suit and the opening lead (against a trump contract) is in some different side suit, where you and the dummy hold length, it is likely to be a singleton. So, too, is a lead of dummy's main side suit.

QUIZ

A.

	♠ 8 ♡ 8 7 5 3 ◇ A K Q 10 7 2 ♣ Q 4
♣2 led	N / W E / S
	♠ A 7 ♡ K Q J 10 6 4 ◇ J 3 ♣ A 10 8

WEST	NORTH	EAST	SOUTH
			1♡
pass	2◇	2♠	4♡
pass	5♡	pass	6♡
all pass			

West leads the ♣2. Which card will you play from dummy?

B.

	♠ 8 5 ♡ A 10 9 3 ◇ A K 2 ♣ J 9 4 2
♠6 led	N / W E / S
	♠ A 9 4 ♡ K 5 2 ◇ Q 7 3 ♣ A K 10 8

West leads the ♠6 against your 3NT game. East plays the queen, which you duck. How would you play if:

i) East returns the ♠2 to West's jack as you duck again. West then plays the ♠7 and East the ♠3 on the third round of the suit.

ii) East returns the ♠10, West's following with the ♠7 as you duck again. East then plays the ♠3 and West follows with the ♠J on the third round of the suit.

Answers

A. East has overcalled in spades, so you would expect West to lead that suit. No doubt he has length in the spade suit and does not expect such a lead to be productive. However, it is surely unthinkable that he has spurned a lead in partner's suit, merely to lead from a jack! It is much more likely that he has led from the club king, hoping to cash two tricks there or to find his partner with the queen. You should therefore rise with dummy's queen of clubs at Trick 1.

B. i) How are the spades divided? Almost certainly, they are 4-4. You can afford to lose the lead to either defender as they have only one more spade winner to cash. Cash one high club, cross to a diamond, and take a club finesse. Even if the finesse loses, you will still make your contract.

ii) How are the spades divided? You must decide which defender holds the ♠2. This is not a situation in which East is likely to false-card at Trick 2. With ♠Q1032 he would surely return his fourth-best spade to give his partner the count. It is much more likely that West is hiding the lowest spade in an attempt to persuade you that it is safe for you to lose the lead to him.

It would be poor play to bank everything on a club finesse into the longer hand. Instead, play a heart to the ten. If this loses, win East's minor-suit return, cash the king of hearts and finesse the heart nine. Only if both heart finesses lose will you have to fall back on the club finesse.

CHAPTER • 3

Counting the Defenders' Shape

Suppose you are in some high contract that depends on a two-way queen guess in a side suit. How would you decide which defender to play for the queen? One possibility is to toss a coin. This will work very well... half the time. A better idea is to seek a count on the defenders' hands.

Let's see how you might obtain such a count.

East-West Vul. Dealer South	♠ A 9 7 ♡ K 8 6 4 ♢ A 10 3 ♣ A 3 2	
♠ J 10 ♡ 10 7 3 ♢ Q 9 8 6 4 2 ♣ Q 4	N W E S	♠ 8 6 5 3 2 ♡ 2 ♢ 7 ♣ J 9 8 7 6 5
	♠ K Q 4 ♡ A Q J 9 5 ♢ K J 5 ♣ K 10	

WEST	NORTH	EAST	SOUTH
			1♡
pass	2NT	pass	4NT
pass	5♢	pass	7♡
all pass			

North's 2NT bid shows a game-forcing heart raise and Blackwood was your obvious next move. Partner's 5♢ response shows four of the five key cards, so you bid the grand slam.

West leads a trump. It takes three rounds to draw trumps, East having begun with a singleton. How would you continue?

You can see twelve top tricks and you will have to guess the two-way diamond finesse for your thirteenth. There are no clues from the bidding or the opening lead to guide you, so which defender will you play for the queen?

If you had to decide now, it would be a 50-50 guess — not very good odds for a grand slam! Fortunately, you don't. Usually the best policy in such situations is to delay the critical decision until as late as possible. By cashing your winners in the other suits, you may pick up some clues to how the diamonds lie. Before doing anything, fix in your mind that West began with three hearts.

Suppose you start by cashing three rounds of spades. East follows all the way, but West discards a diamond on the third round. Ah! Now you can lead a diamond to the ace and finesse against East's diamond queen with confidence. After all, who would discard a diamond if they held the queen?

But what's the rush? Can it cost to cash your club winners and ruff the third round, just in case anything interesting happens? No, and when you do so West follows twice and then discards another diamond as you take your ruff. Well, that confirms it. West might have discarded one diamond if he held the queen, but surely not two...

Are you about to play a diamond to the ace intending to finesse against East on the way back? Of course not, because you have stopped to count the defenders' distribution. Let's recap what we have discovered: West began with three hearts and only two cards in each black suit. He must, therefore, have begun with six diamonds, leaving just a singleton for East.

What started out as a 50-50 contract is now a cast-iron certainty. You cash the diamond king (in case East's singleton is the queen) and lead a second diamond towards dummy. West follows with a low card and you call for the ten knowing with absolute certainty that it will win.

Needless to say, things do not always work quite that well. However, even a little advantage is better than none. Suppose you had discovered, say, that East started with four diamonds and West with only three, the odds would then have been 4-to-3 in favor of East holding the missing queen.

We cannot stress the importance of counting a defender's shape too much. It is a skill that you simply must master if you have aspirations to play this game well. What's more, it's really not that difficult. To see how easy it is, take over the South seat and cover the defenders' cards on this next deal:

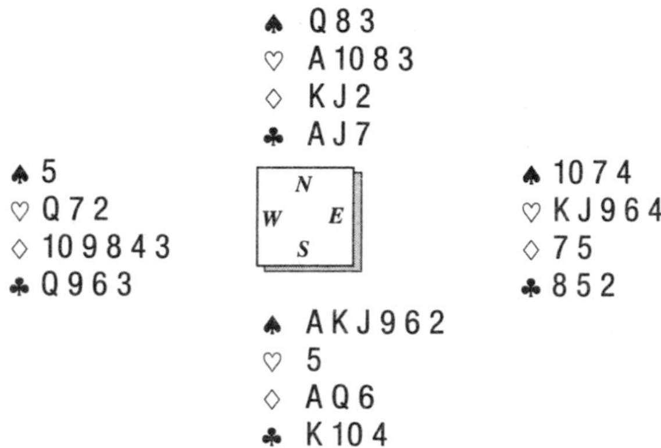

North opens a strong 1NT and you drive to a grand slam in spades. You win the ◇10 lead and draw trumps, noting that East held three cards in the suit. West has thrown two diamonds, meanwhile. What next?

Your next move should be to play on hearts, hoping to gain a count of that suit too. After the ace of hearts and a heart ruff, you cross to the jack of diamonds and ruff another heart. Both defenders follow and, when you return to dummy with the ◇K, East shows out. Make a mental note now that East started with three trumps and two diamonds. When you ruff dummy's last heart the count is complete. West shows out, marking East with 3-5-2-3 shape.

So, you have now found out that West holds four clubs to East's three. This makes him a favorite to hold the club queen. You cash the club king and play a low club to dummy's jack, preparing to bemoan your misfortune should the finesse lose. No, it wins! Sometimes there is justice in this world.

We have asked you to play one or two pretty awful contracts in the first part of this book. The next deal, a 6NT contract, appears to offer no problem at all. Be careful in such a situation. Perhaps a bad break somewhere can still defeat you. (Don't forget to cover the defenders' cards.)

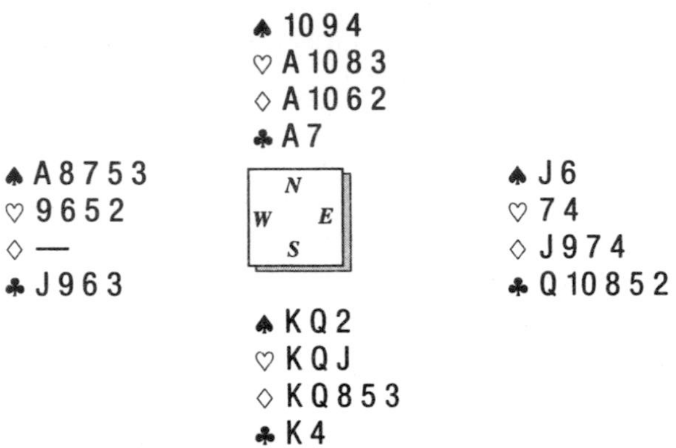

You bid unopposed to 6NT and West favors you with the appalling lead of the ♠5. (This would be sensible against a 3NT contract, but against 6NT a safe heart would have been wiser.) East covers dummy's ten with the jack and you win with the queen. You need a second spade trick, so you immediately return the two of spades. West hops in with his ace and exits with a third spade on which East pitches a club. Are you tempted to claim the rest?

You can almost do so, but there is still one thing that can go wrong — a 4-0 diamond split. Such a division will not necessarily be disastrous, as you can pick up ◇J-9-7-4 in either defender's hand. However, you must cash the correct high honor first. Should you start diamonds by cashing the ace or one of the top cards in your hand?

The answer is that you do not yet know. If either defender holds four diamonds, the 5-2 spade division makes it more likely to be East. Still, it is quite possible that West will hold four diamonds and five spades. Wouldn't you rather delay the decision until you can be 100% sure?

Cashing your heart winners is a good way to start. When you do this, East follows twice and then pitches a club on the third round. So, West began with 5-4 in the majors. You are almost there now, but it is still possible for him to hold four diamonds. Can you see how to be absolutely certain that he does not?

Right, by playing one round of clubs. Be careful, though, which club winner you cash. If East has all four diamonds, you will need a side-suit entry to dummy, so you'd better leave the ace of clubs there. Play a club to the king at this point.

If West shows out on this trick, you will know that he began with four diamonds. You will then start with a high diamond from your hand. As it happens, West follows to the king of clubs. You have now accounted for ten of his cards outside the diamond suit. It is therefore impossible for him to hold four diamonds.

It is time to broach the diamonds, and you are now certain that it is safe to do so by playing towards the ace. Your hard work is rewarded when West discards on this trick. It is easy enough to win the ace of diamonds and lead the ten, covered by the jack and queen. The ace of club remains in dummy so that you can finesse against East's remaining ♢9-x.

Counting the hand may seem like hard work if you have not done it before. It soon becomes automatic and the results can be spectacular. Look at this deal, from a US Vanderbilt final.

North-South Vul. Dealer South	♠ 10 7 6 ♡ 7 4 3 ♢ J 7 3 2 ♣ 10 8 3	
♠ 9 4 ♡ 10 2 ♢ A 9 8 ♣ Q 9 7 5 4 2	N W E S	♠ J 8 3 2 ♡ K Q J 9 8 ♢ 10 6 4 ♣ J
	♠ A K Q 5 ♡ A 6 5 ♢ K Q 5 ♣ A K 6	

WEST	**NORTH**	**EAST**	**SOUTH**
			2♣
pass	2♢	2♡	3NT
all pass			

West led the ♡10 in response to his partner's bid. East overtook and continued the suit, declarer winning the third round. Suppose you had been South, playing in a big national final. How would you have continued?

There is no reason to expect that a count will be useful on this particular hand, but you should nevertheless make a mental note that hearts were 2-5. You will need some diamond tricks, so your next move is to lead the diamond king. West ducks, to prevent you scoring three diamond tricks and East follows with the four, signaling his length. You make a further note that the diamonds appear to be 3-3.

When you continue with the queen of diamonds West ducks again and East plays the six. Yes, the diamonds are surely 3-3. (With something like ◇A-10-9-x, West would probably have taken the ace and knocked out the jack to establish a winner for himself.) The next move is to test your luck in the spade suit. You cash the ace and king but no jack appears. When you play the ♠Q you are interested to note that West shows out.

Do you have a complete count on the hand yet? East started with four spades, five hearts, and three diamonds. So his shape is 4-5-3-1. The data is gathered and now you must use your processing power to calculate a possible route to nine tricks. This is the position you have in fact reached:

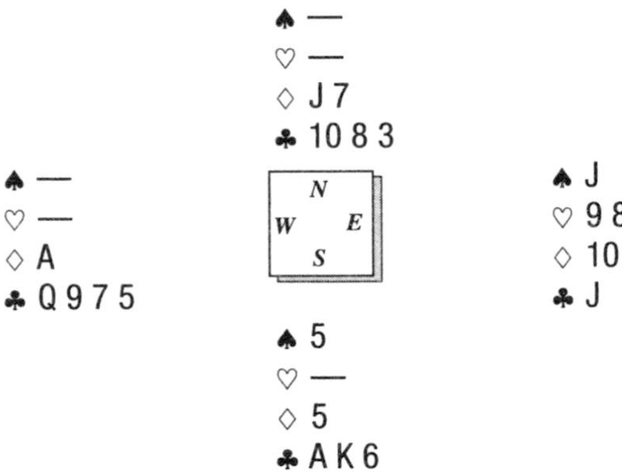

The only chance is that East's singleton club is the queen or jack. You cash the ace of clubs and see the splendid sight of the jack falling on your right. When you continue with a diamond, West is end-played. After winning with the ace, he has to lead away from the ♣Q. You win with dummy's 10 and will actually end up with an overtrick!

Taking advantage of the bidding to read the distribution

In the previous chapter, we saw how the opponents' bidding (or sometimes the lack of it) could help you to place the missing high cards. The bidding can be equally useful when trying to form a picture of the defenders' distribution.

Counting shape will lead you to the right line on the next deal. Cover the defenders' cards and see what you make of it.

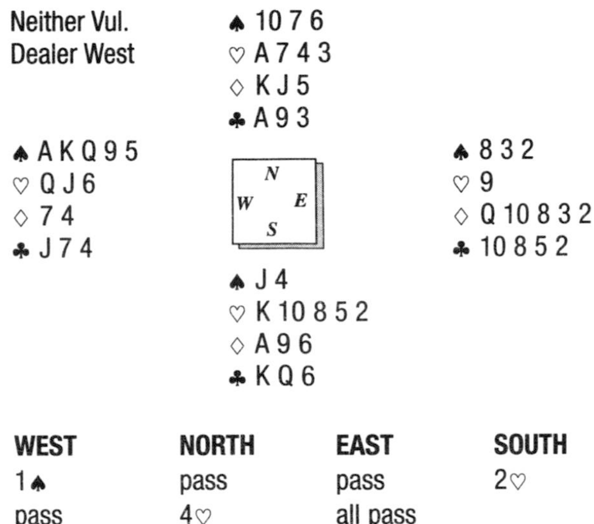

West, whose opening bid promised a five-card suit, leads three top spades against your heart game. East follows all the way and you ruff the third round. When you continue with the ace and king of hearts, East follows with the nine and then discards a diamond on the second round. As West has a sure trump trick, you must now avoid a loser in the diamond suit. Any ideas?

Your first inclination may be that West is likely to hold the queen because he opened the bidding. Whilst this is true, he has already shown up with nine points in spades and three in hearts — enough to justify his opening. Let's see if there are any other clues.

West's opening bid told you that the spades are 5-3. He has since shown up with three hearts, so you know that West has eight cards in the major suits. To put another piece into the jigsaw, you should play your three club winners. When West follows all the way, you have discovered that he can hold at most two diamonds.

The scene is now set for an elimination play. You cash the ace and king of diamonds to leave this position:

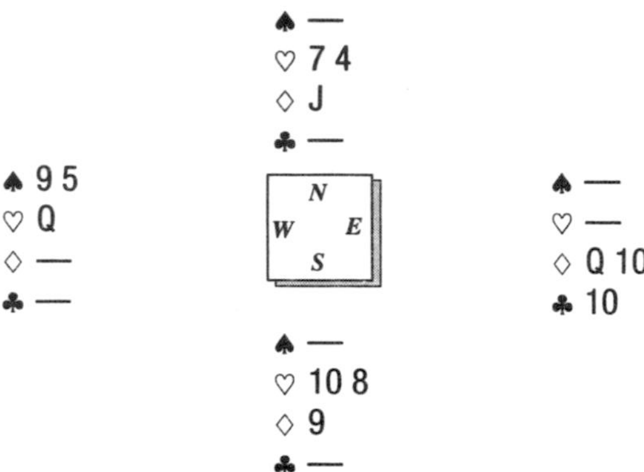

You throw West in with a trump and he has to play a spade, giving you a ruff-and-discard. Away goes your diamond loser and the game is made.

Suppose that West had shown up with two or fewer clubs, which would leave him with at least three diamonds. How would you have played the contract then?

You would have thrown West in with a trump without playing any diamonds first. He would then have been forced to open the diamond suit (or concede a ruff-and-discard). You would have succeeded if West held either the queen of diamonds or the ten.

Bidding on weak, distributional hands can have numerous advantages. For example, doing so will sometimes preempt the opponents out of their best contract or help to locate a cheap sacrifice. Every silver lining has a cloud, though, and if you subsequently become a defender the information given away in the bidding may allow an astute declarer to bring home a contract that would otherwise fail.

Take over from South on the next deal to see if you can take advantage of an opponent's revealing bidding.

Neither Vul.
Dealer South

	North	
	♠ Q J 6 ♡ J 9 3 ◇ A 7 ♣ A J 6 5 3	
West ♠ A 10 8 5 2 ♡ A Q 7 5 2 ◇ 6 ♣ 9 4	N / W E / S	**East** ♠ K 9 3 ♡ 8 6 4 ◇ J 9 8 3 ♣ Q 10 7
	♠ 7 4 ♡ K 10 ◇ K Q 10 5 4 2 ♣ K 8 2	

WEST	NORTH	EAST	SOUTH
			1◇
2◇	3♣	pass	3◇
pass	3♠	dbl	3NT
all pass			

You open 1◇ and West comes in with a Michaels cuebid showing at least 5-5 in the majors. North bids 3♣ and then shows a spade stopper by cuebidding that suit. You decide that your heart stopper justifies a 3NT call, and there matters rest.

West leads the ♠5 to dummy's queen and East's king. You duck the heart switch to West's queen, and he now reverts to spades, cashing the ace and playing a third round. How would you continue?

You will need to bring in one of the minor suits without losing the lead. You have eight cards in each, so which of them should you attack?

Possession of the diamond queen makes that suit the more likely source of tricks. Playing off the top diamonds at this stage would be premature, though. Think back to the bidding — what do you know about the defenders' hands?

You already know that ten of West's cards are in the major suits, leaving him only three in the minors. How can you use this information?

The first thing you should do is to cash the ◇A. (If West discards on this trick, then the chances of a 3-3 club break would be high. You would just have to hope that West's three include the queen.) When West follows to the ◇A, there is no longer any way to score five club tricks, no matter how the defenders' cards are divided. Even so, you are almost home.

Before deciding how to play the diamonds, you must find out how many clubs West holds. So, cash the king and ace of clubs next.

If West discards on either of these tricks, you can conclude that he is likely to hold two or three diamonds. You would then play diamonds from the top, expecting them to divide evenly.

On this occasion, West follows to both top clubs. You now have a complete count on his hand — West must have started with a 5-5-1-2 shape and East with four diamonds to the jack.

Lead dummy's second diamond and put in the ten, fully expecting West to show out. He does so, and when you claim nine tricks you earn a 'Well played' from your partner.

Using the early play to help read the distribution

The opening lead and the early play will often reveal a wealth of information about the hand as a whole. To illustrate, let's say that you are playing in a lowly 1NT contract. West leads the ♠2 at Trick 1, suggesting that he holds only four spades. It is then unlikely that he will hold more than four cards in some other suit. He is most likely to hold a balanced hand, either 4-4-3-2 or 4-3-3-3. Let's imagine next that, at some point early in the play, East gains the lead and switches to a low club. Suppose the hearts you can see are ♡A-6 in dummy and ♡9-8-4 in your hand. What inferences can you draw about the heart suit?

The first is that the suit is surely breaking 4-4. Both defenders have had the chance to open a suit and each has spurned the chance to lead hearts. It is also very likely that the honors are divided — if either defender held something like ♡K-Q-J-x, ♡K-Q-10-x or ♡Q-J-10-x, he may well have preferred to attack hearts in preference to leading a low card in a suit where he obviously needs to find his partner with some help.

On the next deal you must read the lie of the trump suit correctly in order to chose the right line. Various clues are available... if declarer keeps his eyes open. Are you ready to shine?

North-South Vul.
Dealer West

	♠ 7 6 4 2 ♡ A 4 2 ♢ A K 5 ♣ A K Q	
♠ A Q J 9 3 ♡ 10 6 ♢ J 9 3 ♣ 9 6 2	N / W E / S	♠ K 5 ♡ 9 7 5 3 ♢ Q 10 8 ♣ J 10 8 4
	♠ 10 8 ♡ K Q J 8 ♢ 7 6 4 2 ♣ 7 5 3	

WEST	NORTH	EAST	SOUTH
2♠	dbl	pass	3♡
pass	3♠	dbl	4♢
pass	4♡	all pass	

With the vulnerability in his favor, West opens a weak two on a five-card suit. East's subsequent double of 3♠ promises a top honor in the suit and, with the weakness in spades exposed, you end in a 4-3 fit. Remembering his partner's double, West leads a low spade to the king. Back comes a second spade to the jack and West continues with the spade ace, which you are forced to ruff. East discards a club, meanwhile. When you play the king and queen of trumps, West follows with the six and the ten. What next?

If trumps started out 3-3 you can simply cross to the ace of clubs and ruff dummy's last spade with your jack. You can then return to dummy in one or the other minor, draw the last two trumps with dummy's ace and claim the contract. If East started with four trumps, however, this line will fail. East will throw another club when you take your spade ruff and you will not be able to score three club tricks. So, how do the trumps lie?

What shape do you think West has? If he held a minor-suit singleton, he might well have led it. The odds are good that he has some variation of 5-3-3-2 shape. In this case the odds are around 2-to-1 in your favor that West's doubleton is in hearts. It's slightly more than that, in fact. Since your hand and the dummy contain seven cards in each red suit and only six clubs, West's doubleton is less likely to be in clubs than in hearts (or in diamonds).

The early play provides another piece of evidence. West played the ten on the second round of trumps. The Principle of Restricted Choice states that it is more likely that he played the ten because he had to (it was his last card in the suit) than because he chose to play it from his remaining 10-9. This increases even further the probability that West started with only two trumps. (An expert West might cleverly falsecard the 10 from 10-7-6, but we ignore that aspect here.)

So, you abandon the trump suit after two rounds and play three rounds of clubs and two of diamonds. No one ruffs, you are pleased to see, and these cards remain:

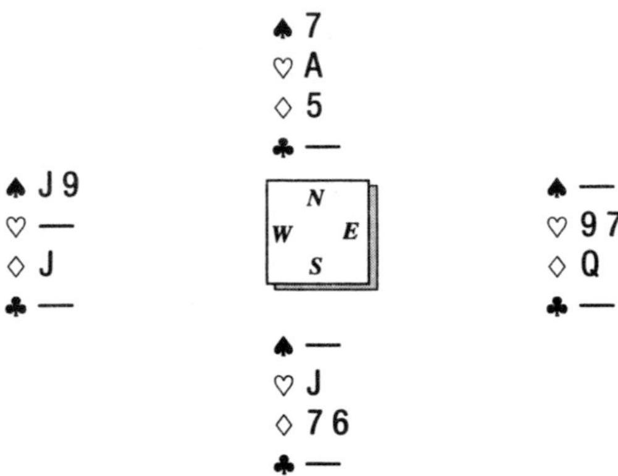

You now lead the ♠7 from dummy, scoring your last two trumps separately.

Key points

1. As declarer, you have two main tasks: to gather information about the defenders' hands and to calculate the best line of play based on this knowledge. By counting the shape of the defenders' hands you can rule out lines of play that would have no chance of success.
2. When a defender has bid, you start with a fair idea of his shape. As the tricks go by, you can refine your count of his hand. For example, you open 1♠ and the next player bids 2NT, the Unusual Notrump showing both minors. If you subsequently play in 4♠ and West leads the ♡8, you would suspect a singleton heart and place him with 2-1-5-5 shape.
3. The opening lead will often tell you how the suit led is breaking, also how the missing honors are distributed.
4. The opening lead and the early play reveal much about the distribution of the defenders' hands. Do not forget to ask yourself what the opening lead tells you about the suits the leader has chosen not to lead. Remember that most players will lead their longest suit against a notrump contract. If the opening lead is from a four-card suit, then the leader is likely to be balanced.
5. When a player makes an opening lead from a dangerous holding, it is likely to be because leads in the other suits were equally or more unattractive. If you have a two-way queen guess in one of the other suits, play the leader for the queen.

A.

♠ A Q 8
♡ K 10 7 3
◇ K 7 2
♣ A 4 2

◇3 led

N
W E
S

♠ K J 6 4
♡ A Q 4
◇ A 8 4
♣ K 7 5

WEST	NORTH	EAST	SOUTH
			1NT
pass	4NT	pass	6NT
all pass			

West leads the ◇3 against your slam. Plan the play.

B.

♠ K 8 5
♡ A 9
◇ Q 10 5 2
♣ Q J 6 2

♠2 led

♠ A 6 4 3
♡ J 2
◇ K 9 3
♣ A K 8 4

WEST	NORTH	EAST	SOUTH
			1NT
pass	3NT	all pass	

West leads the ♠2 against your notrump game. East plays the jack. Plan the play.

Answers

A. You have eleven top tricks and the most likely source of the twelfth is the fourth round of hearts. Essentially, you plan to cash the ace-queen of hearts and lead a third round towards dummy. If the jack has not appeared, you will have to decide between playing the king (hoping for a 3-3 break) or finessing the ten.

With no clues to guide you, the odds are very close. On hands such as this, you must delay your decision until you have seen as many tricks as possible. Indeed, on a good day, you might be able to get a complete count of the hand. It is not good enough to simply play off your winners — a better approach is to win the opening diamond lead and immediately duck a round of clubs. By doing this, you will be able to see three rounds of clubs rather than just two. Suppose the defenders' spades split 3-3 but that West holds only two clubs. If his ♢3 is a true lead, you can then count him for a 3-4-4-2 shape. Assuming that the ♡J does not drop, you will be able to take the finesse with reasonable confidence. If you had not ducked a club, you would never have discovered the layout of that suit.

B. You capture East's jack of spades with the ace at Trick 1 since a heart switch would be a most unwelcome development. Now what?

You have seven top tricks — four clubs, two spades and one heart. You can easily develop an eighth in diamonds and it looks as though the ninth trick will have to come from that suit too. Which defender will you play for the jack of diamonds?

What do you know about the shape of the defenders' hands? The spades are clearly 4-2. What about the hearts? It is a fair bet that East holds at least five hearts, and perhaps even six. West has chosen to lead a broken 4-card spade suit. You can therefore be virtually certain that he does not hold five hearts.

Suppose you play two rounds of clubs and West shows out, discarding a heart, on the second round. Do you now know how the diamonds are breaking? Almost certainly, they are 4-2, West's shape being 4-4-4-1. The odds are therefore 2:1 in favor of West holding the diamond jack. You should lead the first round of the suit from dummy, though — just in case East began with ♢A-J doubleton.

If West captures your king with the ace, he must now switch to a heart to keep the defenders in the ball game. Assuming he does so, you intend to finesse him for the jack of diamonds on the second round.

CHAPTER • 4

Reading the Defenders' Signals

There is one other important source of information for the declarer — the signals that the defenders make. Defenders are forced to signal in many situations, particularly early in the play. It eases their task in defense, yes, but as declarer you can tune in and benefit too.

Many defenders signal their count each time a new suit is broached (high-low to show an even number, low-high to show an odd number). It's a good method, and one that we recommended in our Bridge Technique book, *Defensive Signaling*. As declarer, it is important that you do not let the advantage from this method be all one-way.

Making use of count signals

Perhaps you are skeptical about basing your play on information provided by your opponents. After all, they can elect to signal accurately or they can false-card, and experienced defenders will frequently exercise that choice.

The good news, though, is that many defenders are fairly predictable. For the most part, they can be relied upon to signal honestly when doing so is likely to help their partner. This is particularly true early in the hand, and it is rare that you cannot rely on an opponent's signal at Trick 1.

Suppose this is a side suit in a trump contract:

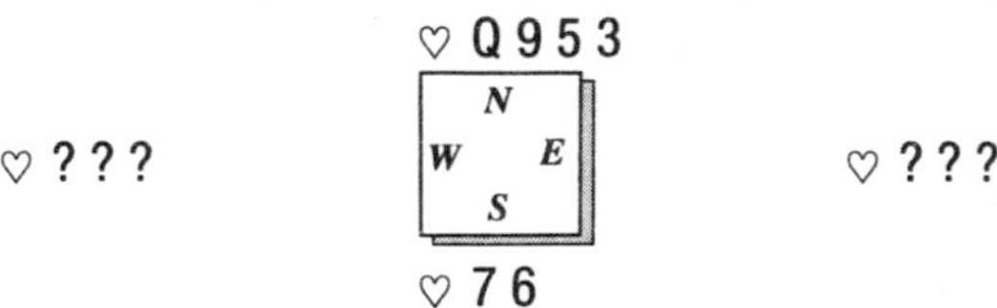

West leads the king of hearts against your contract of four spades. If your opponents' basic signaling method is to show count on their partner's lead, you can be virtually certain that East will play a true card here. Assuming there has been no bidding to suggest that wild distribution exists, you can be fairly sure that the hearts are 4-3 if East follows with the ♡2 at Trick 1. Alternatively, if he plays an obviously high spot (the beginning of a high-low signal), you can be equally certain that the suit is either 5-2 or 3-4.

Such information may prove vital later in the hand, when you are trying to get a complete count. This is particularly true when the suit led is one in which you hold relatively few cards (eg. Axx opposite a singleton), and you can never play enough rounds of the suit for a defender to show out.

However, good defenders are also very quick to recognize when a signal is more likely to help declarer than their partner. For example:

Declaring a notrump contract, suppose you play a spade to the ace and the defenders follow with the three and the two — the lowest of the missing spades. Would it be reasonable to assume that the spades are splitting 3-3 because each defender has started a low-high signal?

No, because it is clear to both defenders that knowing how many spades they hold is unlikely to be of any great advantage to their partner.

As a defender, you must learn to recognize when you need to signal accurately and when you can simply follow suit or even attempt to muddy the waters with a false signal. Signal too little, and you constantly leave your partner guessing what to do. Overdo it, and you become a patsy for a watchful declarer.

Similarly, as declarer, it is important that you recognize the various situations, so that you can look at them from the defender's point of view. Having realized when a defender is likely to signal accurately, it becomes a relatively simple matter to place him in situations where he must signal. Consider this layout:

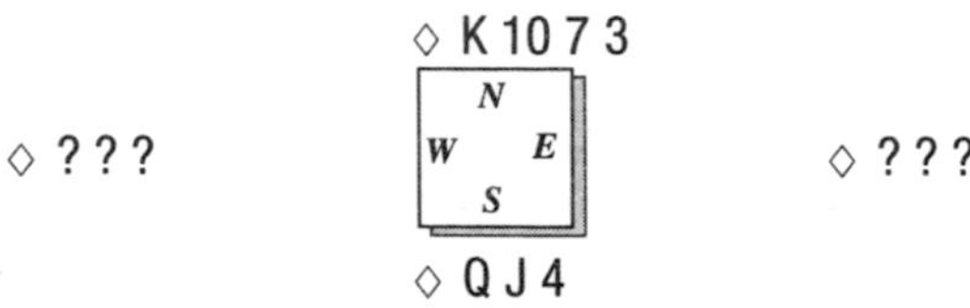

Suppose you are playing a no-trump contract with this diamond suit. When you lead the queen, the defenders are very likely to signal their length honestly. (This is particularly true if dummy has no obvious entry.) A defender looking at some number of low diamonds must signal accurately so that his partner knows when to take the ace. In this case, he will need to hold up until the third round to prevent you from reaching your third winner in the suit. If, instead, you held ◇Q-J doubleton, then the defender with the ace wants to jump on the second round of the suit, limiting you to one diamond trick.

To get these and many similar situations right with any consistency, defenders must be able to rely on accurate count signals from their partner. As declarer, you can make use of these situations in which experienced defenders are almost guaranteed to signal honestly.

Suppose instead that your diamond suit looks something like this:

◇ K 10 7 3

◇ ? ? ? N W E S ◇ ? ? ?

◇ A Q 4

Again, you are in a notrump contract with no outside entry to dummy. This time, of course, you don't need a side-suit entry as you can get to dummy with the diamond king. The crucial question this time is whether the diamonds are breaking 3-3 or whether West holds jack fourth. It would be nice, would it not, if the defenders could be encouraged to tell you the answer to this question? They can!

Notice the enormous difference it makes whether you start this suit by laying down the ace or by advancing the queen. It makes no material difference, of course, but if you start with the ace then the defenders will simply follow suit with the card nearest their thumb and you will discover nothing. If you start with the queen, though, the defenders are likely to signal their count accurately in case partner holds the ace. This will greatly assist you when you have to guess what to do on the third round of diamonds.

There is one further point relating to the play of this suit that is worth stressing. Throughout this book, we have discussed the importance of leaving critical decisions until as late as possible. The defenders, of course, would like to be able to do the same thing. As declarer, you control the tempo of the hand, and part of your strategy should be to force the defenders into decisions early in the hand. With this diamond suit, you want the defenders to signal accurately. If you wait until the late stages of the hand before leading the queen of diamonds, you are unlikely to get any reliable information. By then, the defenders will know what is going on and they will have no need to signal. Ideally, you should lead the diamond queen very early — as soon as you get to your hand would be best.

Making use of attitude and suit-preference signals

What reliance should you place on the defenders' signals when they are discarding? Once again you should treat them as honest cards when made early in the play.

For example, suppose you are declaring a lowly two spade contract. When you draw trumps, West pitches an encouraging club. You have two small clubs in the dummy and ♣K-J-x in your hand. Of course, West may be signaling for a club switch because he has both the ace and the queen, which will not help you at all. When the time comes for you to guess the clubs, though, you should be much more inclined to place West with the ace than with the queen. The one thing of which you can be certain is that both club honors are not onside, so if playing for that was one of your options, forget it and look elsewhere. Defenders simply do not signal encouragement in suits where they hold four small cards.

Defenders only very rarely give false suit-preference signals. Take a look at the next deal:

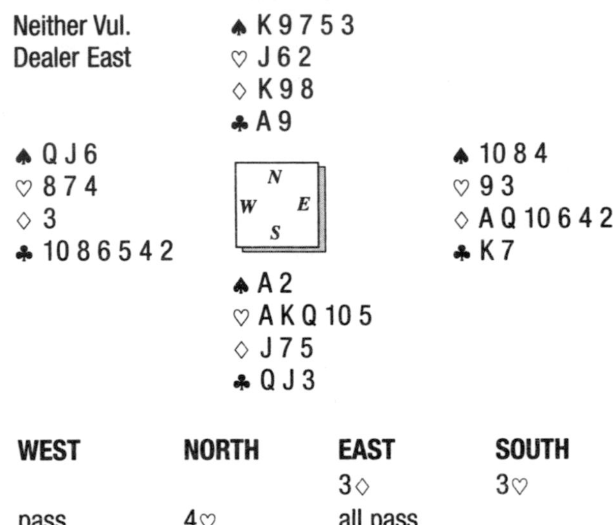

WEST	NORTH	EAST	SOUTH
		3◇	3♡
pass	4♡	all pass	

West leads the diamond three. East takes two tricks in the suit and returns the two of diamonds for his partner to ruff. West then produces the five of clubs — decision time!

How do you assess the various chances? There are two alternatives. One is the club finesse, which, after East's preempt, rates to be better than a 50-50 shot. The other is to play for a 3-3 spade break.

The odds on a 3-3 spade break are far worse than 50%, particularly when the diamonds are known to be 6-1. Why, then, should you eschew the finesse in favor of this much poorer chance?

Think about East's signal. He had a choice of diamonds to return at Trick 3, but he chose the two, a clear suit-preference signal for a club. He could have chosen either the ten to ask for a spade or the four or six which would have been neutral cards.

What are the chances that East has asked for a club switch to deter you from taking a winning finesse in the suit?

Almost none — asking for a club when he held nothing in the suit would be incredibly dangerous. From East's point of view, his partner might hold the king-jack, and a club switch around to your unsupported queen might be the only way to let the contract make. No, the only explanation for East asking for a club switch is that he holds the king.

You should rise with the ♣A, draw two rounds of trumps, and play three rounds of spades, ruffing. When the spades split 3-3, you can cross to the jack of trumps and discard your club losers on the long spades — contract made!

Inferences from the first discard

Whether or not it is the best strategy on a particular hand, nearly all defenders make the 'easy' discards first. If they have to find a discard from five hearts and four clubs, they will throw a heart first. If they are forced to make further discards later, they will calculate more closely which suit to throw and which to keep. Knowing that this is the way defenders operate will assist you in counting the hand as declarer.

Cover the defenders' hands on the next deal and see if you would read the contents of the West hand correctly.

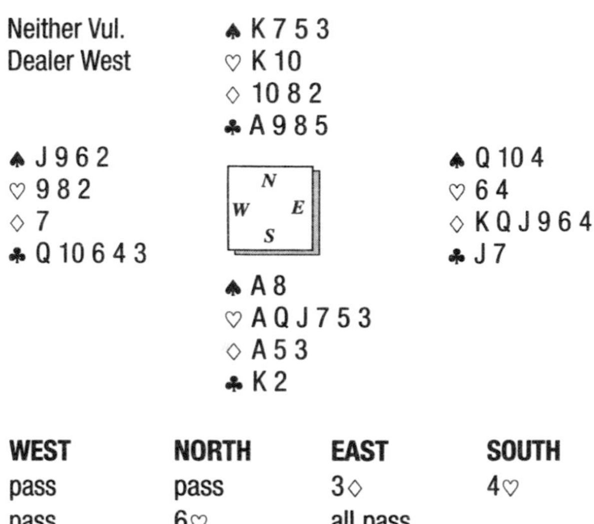

WEST	NORTH	EAST	SOUTH
pass	pass	3◇	4♡
pass	6♡	all pass	

You don't admire the bidding? Maybe not, but suppose you are South and are faced with the task of scoring twelve tricks. West leads the ◇7 and you take East's jack with the ace. The only apparent chance is to squeeze West in the black suits. You draw trumps in three rounds, throwing a diamond from dummy. When you continue with a fourth trump, West discards a club and you dispose of dummy's last diamond. Now comes a fifth round of trumps; West considers for a while and then throws a spade. What will you discard from dummy?

West started with nine cards in the black suits and has thrown one card in each suit. He must therefore have reduced to only three cards in one of the black suits. If you can guess which one, you can discard from dummy in the other suit and ruff a long card good in the first suit. Against all but a very top-class defender you can be confident that

West's first discard, a club, came from his five-card suit. You should therefore throw a club from dummy, ruff a long spade good, and return to enjoy it with the club ace. Well bid, partner!

You were able to bring this contract home because of West's ill-judged choice of first discard. Had he thrown a spade on the fourth round of trumps, then a club, you would almost certainly have mis-read the position, thrown the wrong black suit from dummy and gone one down.

Is the defender in trouble?

The tempo of your opponents' discarding may be the tell-tale key that leads you to the winning line of play in a squeeze or an endplay situation. The lessons of the next deal are twofold: as declarer, always be aware of an opponent's bearing and tempo. If a defender seems to be in trouble, ask yourself why. The answer will frequently lead you to the realization that he can be squeezed or endplayed.

Secondly, when you are defending, take time early in the play to develop an overall plan. Do not wait until you are struggling to find a good discard. Doing this only tells declarer that you are in trouble.

A common situation occurs when declarer starts to run a long suit. You will soon know how many times you are going to have to discard. Pause as early in the play as possible, select the appropriate number of discards, and then decide the order in which to make those discards based on how best to disguise your (or your partner's) holding.

Take over from South and see how you fare on this deal:

North-South Vul. Dealer South	♠ A Q 5 ♡ A J 3 ◇ 8 4 ♣ J 8 6 5 4	
♠ J 10 9 ♡ 8 ◇ A Q J 10 9 3 ♣ K 7 3	N W E S	♠ 8 7 6 4 3 ♡ 9 2 ◇ 7 6 5 ♣ 10 9 2
	♠ K 2 ♡ K Q 10 7 6 5 4 ◇ K 2 ♣ A Q	

WEST	NORTH	EAST	SOUTH
			1♡
2◇	3◇	pass	4NT
pass	5♡	pass	6♡
all pass			

North's three diamonds cuebid showed a sound heart raise. After using Blackwood to check that there are not two aces missing, you install yourself in the small slam. West leads the jack of spades. How would you play?

You have eleven tricks and a choice of minor-suit finesses for a twelfth trick. However, West's overcall suggests that neither the ace of diamonds nor the king of clubs is likely to be favorably placed for you. A 'strip and endplay' appears to be the best option.

Suppose you win the opening lead in hand with the spade king, draw trump, and cash your spade winners discarding a diamond from your hand. When you then run the trumps, the four-card end position will look something like this:

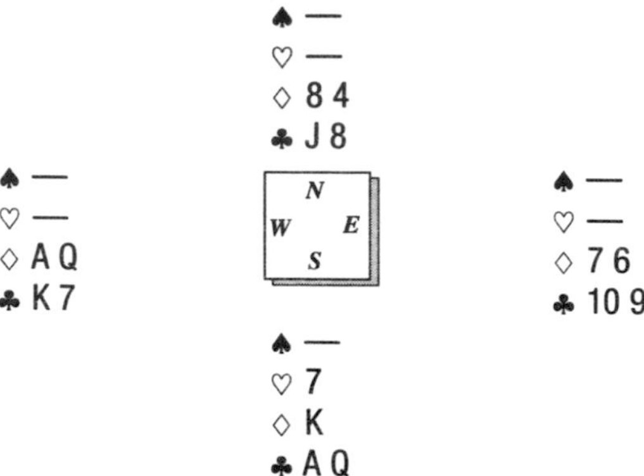

When you cash the final trump, West has a choice of losing options. If he discards the queen of diamonds, you will exit with the diamond king to his ace; he will have to lead into your club tenace. Alternatively, if he throws a club, you will cash the ace, dropping his king, and score your twelfth trick with the club queen.

Most defenders in the West seat will come down to the four cards shown in the diagram. Some will then huff and puff before finally choosing a discard. Against those defenders, do you think you will have any problem working out which of their honors is now singleton?

These defenders made all of their easy discards early. When they had to make the really tough discard, you were alert and watchful. There is nothing West can do to stop you making this contract. He can, however, make it much more difficult.

An experienced defender in the West seat will foresee the end position. He will discard his one or two low clubs early in the hand. His last four cards will be something like ♢A-Q-9 ♣K. When he then discards the queen of diamonds on the last trump, you will have to guess whether he has bared his ace of diamonds or the king of clubs.

You may think that the answer to this type of problem is to watch West's cards very carefully. In fact, the key player here is probably East. Holding nothing of value, many defenders in the East seat will consider it their duty to signal accurately to tell their partner how to defend. You must watch East's cards like a hawk. It is from East that you will usually learn how the minor suits are distributed. Once you have that information, there is nothing West can do to deflect you from the winning play.

In closing this chapter, we should mention that it is important for you to familiarize yourself with the opponents' defensive methods. For example, suppose you come across a situation in which you can get a count of a suit because the defenders have to signal honestly. The information gained is of no use to you if you do not know whether your opponents are playing standard signaling methods. If you have to ask 'what does that card mean?' during the play, you not only alert the opponents to a signal that may have been missed, but you also tip the defenders off that you are paying attention.

In an IMPs match, make sure you understand your opponents' basic signaling methods before you start the first deal against them. Playing a pairs event, take a moment to check the methods, as shown on your opponents' convention card, as soon as you become declarer. This is something that can easily be done while LHO is considering his opening lead.

Key points

1. The opening lead and signals given early in the play are usually honest. You can treat information gleaned from such signals as reliable.

2. Always try to view a problem from the defender's angle. You will often see that he cannot afford to play a deceptive card, as doing so risks leading his partner astray. In such circumstances, you can treat a signal from that defender as honest.

3. A defender who holds all of his side's assets will rarely bother to signal. After all, his partner, who has virtually nothing, does not need to know which of his thirteen small cards to keep — they are all irrelevant. A defender whose hand is known to be very weak will tend to signal accurately.

4. If you need the defenders to tell you how a suit is breaking, lead the suit early. If you wait until later in the hand, when the defenders already know all they need about the layout, they will not bother to signal. You will therefore gain no useful information from their carding.

5. Opponents who play attitude signals will often give you a blueprint to the missing honors. Suit-preference signals can also be used to similar ends.

QUIZ

A.

♠ 8 4 2
♡ K Q 10 3
◇ 7 2
♣ 8 7 3 2

♠3 led

N / W E / S

♠ K Q J
♡ A 7 4
◇ A Q J 10
♣ Q J 5

WEST	NORTH	EAST	SOUTH
			2NT
pass	3♣	pass	3♦
pass	3NT	all pass	

You win East's ♠10 with the jack. After a heart to the king, you take a losing diamond finesse. West plays ace and another spade, East following twice. Plan the play.

B.

♠ K 8 4 3
♡ A J 7 4 2
◇ A 5 2
♣ 6

♠2 led

N / W E / S

♠ A
♡ K Q 10 9 3
◇ K J 10 3
♣ A 7 4

WEST	NORTH	EAST	SOUTH
			1♥
pass	4♣	pass	4NT
pass	5♥	pass	7♥
all pass			

You win East's ♠J with the ace. You lay down the ♡K and East discards a diamond. When you continue drawing trumps, East thinks for some time and then pitches two spades. You can ruff your club losers and throw one diamond on the ♠K, but you will have to guess the two-way diamond position. Which defender will you play for the ◇Q?

Answers

A. You need four heart tricks to make the contract and the defenders' spot cards on the first round of this suit may assist you to guess correctly. Suppose when you lead a heart to the king at Trick 2, West follows with the ♡2 and East with the ♡8. Remember those spot cards! When you later cash the ♡A, let's say West follows with the ♡5 and East with the ♡6. That's interesting — one defender has played upwards and the other other has followed high-low. One of them is lying!

Almost certainly, West holds J-9-5-2 and did not signal his length because the approaching guess for declarer was apparent. East holds 8-6 and did signal his length, since partner might hold the ace and would need to know how many times he should hold up. You should therefore finesse on the third round of hearts.

If instead both defenders followed upwards in hearts, you would play for a 3-3 break.

B. What do you make of East's early diamond discard?

The opening lead tells you that spades are likely to be 4-4. That leaves East with nine cards in the minors. How do you think those nine cards are distributed? If East held four or fewer diamonds, wouldn't he have had plenty of clubs to throw? His 'easy' diamond discard surely marks him with 4-0-5-4 shape.

If East began with five diamonds, that leaves only a singleton for West. You should play a diamond to the ace and finesse against East on the way back. If West follows at all to the second round of diamonds, it will be a surprise.

More Bridge Titles from Master Point Press

ABTA Book of the Year Award winners

25 Bridge Conventions You Should Know
by Barbara Seagram and Marc Smith (foreword by Eddie Kantar)
192pp., PB Can $19.95 US$ 15.95

Eddie Kantar teaches Modern Bridge Defense
Eddie Kantar teaches Advanced Bridge Defense
by Eddie Kantar
each 240pp., PB Can $27.95 US$ 19.95

Also available in Interactive CD-ROM Editions

Modern Bridge Defense Can $69.95, US$ 49.95
Advanced Bridge Defense Can $69.95, US$ 49.95

Around the World in 80 Hands by Zia Mahmood with David Burn
256pp., PB Can $22.95 US $16.95

A Study in Silver *A second collection of bridge stories*
by David Silver
128pp., PB Can $12.95 US$ 9.95

Becoming a Bridge Expert by Frank Stewart
300pp., PB Can $27.95 US $19.95

Bridge Problems for a New Millennium by Julian Pottage
160pp., PB Can $14.95 US $14.95

Bridge the Silver Way by David Silver and Tim Bourke
192pp., PB Can $19.95 US $14.95

Bridge: 25 Ways to Compete in the Bidding.
by Barbara Seagram and Marc Smith
220pp., PB Can.$19.95 US $15.95

Bridge, Zia... and me by Michael Rosenberg
(foreword by Zia Mahmood)
192pp., PB Can $19.95 US $15.95

Challenge Your Declarer Play by Danny Roth
128pp., PB Can. $12.95 US $ 9.95

Classic Kantar *a collection of bridge humor* by Eddie Kantar
192pp., PB Can $19.95 US $14.95

Competitive Bidding in the 21st Century by Marshall Miles
254pp.,PB Can. $22.95 US. $16.95

Countdown to Winning Bridge by Tim Bourke and Marc Smith
92pp., PB Can $19.95 US $14.95

Easier Done Than Said *Brilliancy at the Bridge Table*
by Prakash K. Paranjape
128pp., PB Can $15.95 US $12.95

For Love or Money *The Life of a Bridge Journalist*
by Mark Horton and Brian Senior
189pp., PB Can $22.95 US $16.95

Focus On Declarer Play by Danny Roth
128pp., PB Can $12.95 US $9.95

Focus On Defence by Danny Roth
128pp., PB Can $12.95 US $9.95

Focus On Bidding by Danny Roth
160pp., PB Can $14.95 US $11.95

I Shot my Bridge Partner by Matthew Granovetter
384pp., PB Can $19.95 US $14.95

Murder at the Bridge Table by Matthew Granovetter
320pp., PB Can $19.95 US $14.95

Partnership Bidding *a workbook* by Mary Paul
96pp., PB Can $9.95 US $7.95

Playing with the Bridge Legends by Barnet Shenkin
(forewords by Zia and Michael Rosenberg)
240pp., PB Can $24.95 US $17.95

Saints and Sinners T*he St. Titus Bridge Challenge*
by David Bird & Tim Bourke
192pp., PB Can $19.95 US $14.95

Samurai Bridge *A tale of old Japan* by Robert F. MacKinnon
256pp., PB Can $ 22.95 US $16.95

Tales out of School *'Bridge 101'* and other stories by David Silver
(foreword by Dorothy Hayden Truscott)
128pp., PB Can $ 12.95 US $9.95

The Best of Bridge Today Online by Matthew and Pamela Granovetter
192pp., PB Can $ 19.95 US $14.95

The Bridge Magicians by Mark Horton and Radoslaw Kielbasinski
248pp., PB Can $24.95 US $17.95

The Bridge Player's Bedside Book edited by Tony Forrester
256pp., HC Can $27.95 US $19.95

The Complete Book of BOLS Bridge Tips edited by Sally Brock
176pp., PB (photographs) Can $24.95 US$17.95

There Must Be A Way… *52 challenging bridge hands*
by Andrew Diosy (foreword by Eddie Kantar)
96pp., PB $9.95 US & Can.

Thinking on Defense by Jim Priebe
192pp., PB Can $19.95 US $15.95

You Have to See This… *52 more challenging bridge problems*
by Andrew Diosy and Linda Lee
96pp., PB Can $12.95 US $9.95

Win the Bermuda Bowl with me by Jeff Meckstroth and Marc Smith
188pp., PB Can $24.95 US $17.95

World Class — *conversations with the bridge masters*
by Marc Smith
288pp., PB (photographs) Can $24.95 US $17.95